SPIES AND TRAITORS

STORIES OF MASTERS OF DECEPTION

by Michael Burgan

CAPSTONE PRESS
a capstone imprint

Velocity is published by Capstone Press,
151 Good Counsel Drive, P.O. Box 669, Mankato, Minnesota 56002.
www.capstonepress.com

092009
005620LKS10

Books published by Capstone Press are manufactured with paper containing at least 10 percent post-consumer waste.

Library of Congress Cataloging-in-Publication Data
Burgan, Michael.
    Spies and traitors : stories of masters of deception / by Michael Burgan.
    p. cm. — (Velocity. Bad guys)
    Summary: "Provides short biographies of some of the world's most infamous spies and traitors, detailing their criminal ways" — Provided by publisher.
    Includes bibliographical references and index.
    ISBN 978-1-4296-3424-3 (library binding)
    1. Espionage — Juvenile literature. 2. Spies — Juvenile literature. I. Title.
UB270.5.B869 2010
327.120092'2 — dc22
                                               2009026656

Photo Credits

AP Images/Bob Daugherty, 34; Denis Paquin, 42; Doug Mills, 41
The Bridgeman Art Library/Look and Learn/Private Collection, 6 (bottom)
Corbis/Bettmann, 21, 26, 32, 35, 36; Fifty, NT, 40; Fine Art Photographic Library, 8 (bottom)
Courtesy of Army Art Collection, U.S. Army Center of Military History, 11, 15
Courtesy of the Federal Bureau of Investigations, 38 (badge)
DVIC/NARA, 14, 23
Getty Images Inc., 45; Alexandria County Sheriffs Department, 44 (top); Hulton Archive/Keystone, 22 (both), 24 (both); Newsmakers/FBI, 37 (front); Time Life Pictures/FBI, 43; Time Life Pictures/Gjon Mili, 20; Time Life Pictures/Grey Villet, cover (Hiss); Time Life Pictures/J. R. Eyerman, 29; Time Life Pictures/Mansell, 13; Time Life Pictures/William Vandivert, 19
iStockphoto/princess35, 17 (left)
Library of Congress, 9, 12, 16 (front), 17 (right), 18 (top and bottom), 28, 31 (bottom), 44 (bottom)
National Archives and Records Administration, 16 (bottom)
Newscom/AFP Photo/Paul J. Richards, 39
Shutterstock/antloft, 10 (right); bioraven, 5 (right), 37 (back); Dan Lee, 5 (left); Doug Priebe, 31 (top); FilipHerzig, 4 (front); Ian O'Hanlon, cover (film strip); Igor Kaliuzhnyi, 38 (diamonds); Jeff Carpenter, 17 (bullets); JustASC, 4 (back), 16 (back); Lance Bellers, 25; Martin D. Vonka, 7 (Parthenon); Mushakesa, 18 (bullet hole); Myotis, 8 (top); Olemac, 6 (top); PeJo, 33; Terekhov Igor, 27 (bottom)
Wikimedia/Public Domain, 10 (left)
Wikipedia, public-domain image, 7 (bust), 27 (top); National Archives and Record Administration, 30

Design Elements

Library of Congress (map); Shutterstock/Hintau Aliaksei (tape); Shutterstock/Ian O'Hanlon (film); Shutterstock/Nassyrov Ruslan (photo frames); Shutterstock/Picsfive (push pins); Shutterstock/Vasyl Helevachuk (picture frame)

Capstone Press thanks Jason Palson (pseudonym), former member of the Air Force Office of Special Investigations, for his help with this book. Mr. Palson thanks the brave men and women of the Air Force Office of Special Investigations for their work to thwart those who wish to do harm to the United States and her allies.

TABLE OF CONTENTS

BAD APPLES

When it comes to traitors, the old saying, "Every bushel has a bad apple," is dead on. While most people are honest, some are rotten at the core. They turn against their homelands to help other nations or groups. They become traitors who break the trust of others and commit harmful acts of **treason**.

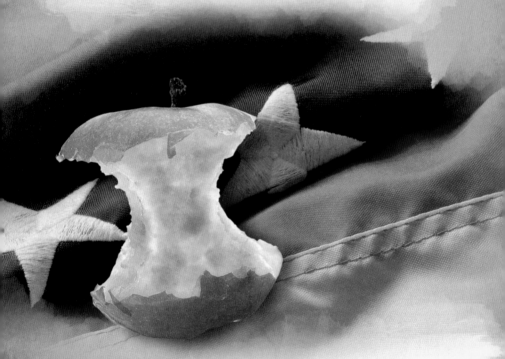

Many spies help their countries. They help protect their countries by secretly watching the actions of enemy countries. They also gather secret information to bring down unjust leaders around the world.

treason

the crime of betraying your country by spying for another country or by helping an enemy during a war

But a few spies cross the line between helping their country and betraying it. They trade information to other countries for profit. They pretend to be good citizens while they actually work against their country.

Becoming a spy or a traitor carries the risk of jail or death. With such high stakes, why do they do it? A big reason might be the money. Spies and traitors are usually paid for their work. The chance to make a ton of cash might be too tempting to turn down. But money may not be the only reason. Some spies and traitors believe their country is doing something wrong. They think their treason will help fix it. Whatever their reasons, you're about to meet some of the worst spies and traitors who ever lived.

marcus junius Brutus

85 BC – 42 BC

Starting in 49 BC, two powerful Roman generals fought a bloody civil war. Julius Caesar won and took control of the Roman Empire. Marcus Junius Brutus had been a Roman soldier who opposed the new ruler. His hatred grew so strong that he turned against Caesar and helped kill him.

painting of Caesar's murder

Brutus had fought Caesar's forces during the civil war. But after the war, Caesar forgave Brutus and wanted his support. Caesar gave him the powerful job of senator in the new government. He considered Brutus a friend.

Caesar hoped to improve education, construct new buildings, and make the Roman government run smoother. But Brutus and other senators believed that Caesar was destroying Rome.

On March 15, 44 BC, Brutus and a group of senators killed Caesar. Soon after, Brutus fled Rome. He killed himself two years later. To some people, he had saved Rome from a terrible ruler. To others, he was a traitor who helped kill a skilled leader.

bust of Marcus Junius Brutus

FACT:

In William Shakespeare's play about Julius Caesar, the dying ruler says, "Et tu, Brute?" It means, "You too, Brutus?" Today, some people use this saying when someone they trusted has betrayed them.

JUDAS ISCARIOT

? – 30 AD

In the Bible, Judas Iscariot was one of 12 **disciples** who traveled with Jesus Christ. He is also one of the most infamous traitors of all time.

disciple

someone who follows the teachings of a leader

When Jewish leaders wanted Jesus executed, Judas agreed to betray him. No one really knows why Judas turned against his teacher and friend. But in return for his betrayal, he would receive 30 pieces of silver.

On the night of the betrayal, Jesus shocked his disciples by saying one of them would soon turn against him. None of the disciples could believe there was a traitor among them.

Later that night, Judas carried out his plan. He kissed Jesus in front of the Jewish leaders. The kiss meant that Jesus was the man they should arrest.

Today, details of Judas' story serve as symbols of the acts of traitors. These include taking 30 pieces of silver for betraying someone and using a kiss to mark someone for arrest.

FACT:

One Bible writer says Judas felt horrible about his betrayal of Jesus. He gave back the money he received and hung himself. Others say he used the money to buy land that was later called the Field of Blood.

BENEDICT ARNOLD

1741 – 1801

When the Revolutionary War (1775–1783) began, Benedict Arnold eagerly joined the battle against Great Britain. By the end of the war, he was one of the most hated men in America.

Arnold began his military career as leader of Connecticut's volunteer army, or militia. By 1777, he was a general who showed great bravery and skill on the battlefield. But Arnold was eager to win fame. Some U.S. leaders thought he risked the lives of his men to gain glory for himself. Arnold became upset when other officers were promoted before him. He also argued with Congress over money. Arnold claimed he was not paid what he was owed.

In 1778, Arnold became the military commander in Philadelphia. At the same time, he grew friendly with local **loyalists**. Arnold even married the daughter of a loyalist.

Some **patriots** in the city disliked his ties to the loyalists. They also thought he used his position to make money illegally. In 1780, Arnold was accused of breaking several laws. He was found guilty of two charges.

loyalist

a colonist who was loyal to Great Britain during the Revolutionary War

patriot

a person who sided with the colonists during the Revolutionary War

Arnold only received a slight punishment, but he was still angry. He believed he had not done anything wrong and hadn't deserved to be punished. As revenge, Arnold decided to help the British fight the Americans.

Arnold secretly contacted the British. He offered to get the command of West Point, a major fort in upstate New York. After gaining control, he would turn over the fort to British troops in return for money. The British agreed.

THE CAPTURE OF ANDRE.

By John Paulding, David Williams and Isaac Van Wart, at Tarrytown, N.Y. Sept. 23rd 1780.

Arnold arrived at West Point in August 1780. Soon he met with British Major John Andre. Arnold gave Andre papers with important information about the fort and its troops.

After the meeting, Andre was caught by members of the local militia. They found the papers Arnold had given him. The patriots sent the papers to General George Washington.

Arnold learned about Andre's arrest and fled. He headed for a British ship anchored in the Hudson River. The British took him aboard and gave him command of troops to fight the Americans.

FACT:

To send messages to the British, Arnold wrote in a secret code. He and Andre both had copies of a well-known book. If Arnold wrote the numbers "293.9.7," Andre knew to turn to page 293 of the book and look for the seventh word in the ninth line.

Arnold soon raided the town of New London, Connecticut. His troops destroyed a ship filled with gunpowder. The powder sparked a fire that burned many buildings in the city. Arnold's forces also killed American soldiers after they surrendered at a nearby fort.

After the war, many British did not trust Arnold. He had already betrayed one country. They could not be sure he would not betray another. Arnold spent his last years in England and Canada. He never returned to the United States. Today, Americans still call someone who is disloyal or a traitor a "Benedict Arnold."

Britain's Spymaster

John Andre was in charge of British spying during the Revolutionary War. He recruited Americans to spy for the British. Andre became friendly with Benedict Arnold's future wife. When Arnold decided to become a traitor, she arranged contact between him and Andre. When Andre was captured in 1780, he was pretending to be a merchant named John Anderson. He admitted he was actually a British officer. He was hung as a spy.

JAMES WILKINSON

1757 – 1825

James Wilkinson led a life full of secrecy. During the Revolutionary War, Wilkinson won a promotion many soldiers believed he didn't deserve. After the war, he tried to gain money and fame at any cost. Many of his deeds have been forgotten, but he was one of the United States' worst traitors.

In 1787, Wilkinson secretly began working for Spain while he lived in Kentucky. At that time, Kentucky belonged to the United States but was not yet a state. Spain controlled the Louisiana Territory to the west.

Wilkinson wanted to help the Spanish take Kentucky and add it to their lands. Wilkinson pledged loyalty to the Spanish king and took money from Spain. These were acts of treason. He kept working for Spain even after rejoining the U.S. Army in 1791.

In 1803, Louisiana joined the United States. Wilkinson was soon named its governor. Two years later, he and former vice president Aaron Burr planned to form a new country centered in Louisiana. Before they could act, Wilkinson turned in Burr. The government tried to find out if Wilkinson was part of the **conspiracy**, but he was not charged.

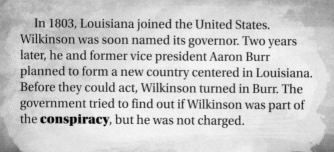

Aaron Burr

Suspicions about Wilkinson's past continued. In 1811, he faced a court-martial because of his service to Spain. But Wilkinson convinced the court he was innocent. Years later historians found documents that proved his guilt.

FACT:

During the Revolutionary War, Wilkinson left a job after people suspected him of taking money for himself.

conspiracy
a secret, illegal plan that a group of people makes

1838 – 1865

John Wilkes Booth hated President Abraham Lincoln. He also hated the Union's defeat of the Confederacy during the Civil War (1861–1865). Booth wanted to bring down the U.S. government. Killing Lincoln was part of his plan.

In 1861, the Confederate states feared President Lincoln would end slavery. Booth and many Southerners believed the states had a legal right to allow slavery. Booth also believed the president denied citizens' legal rights and allowed mistreatment of Southern prisoners during the war. Booth thought it was his duty to end Lincoln's presidency any way he could.

At first, Booth wanted to kidnap the president. But in March 1865, Booth realized the South would lose the war. Booth and several people planned to kill Lincoln and two other government leaders.

On April 14, Lincoln went to a play at Ford's Theatre in Washington, D.C. Booth was a well-known actor. He easily got past a guard close to the president. Standing just a few feet from Lincoln, Booth fired a pistol at the back of Lincoln's head. Then he jumped from the seats down to the stage. He ran out of the building and took off on a waiting horse. President Lincoln died early the next morning.

FACT:

Lewis Powell took part in the plan to kill government leaders. Powell went to the home of Secretary of State William Seward. He stabbed Seward and injured two other men, but none of them died.

SURRATT.   BOOTH.   HAROLD.

War Department, Washington, April 20, 1865,

$100,000 REWARD!

THE MURDERER

Of our late beloved President, Abraham Lincoln,

IS STILL AT LARGE.

$50,000 REWARD

Will be paid by this Department for his apprehension, in addition to any reward offered by Municipal Authorities or State Executives.

$25,000 REWARD

Will be paid for the apprehension of JOHN H. SURRATT, one of Booth's Accomplices.

$25,000 REWARD

Will be paid for the apprehension of David C. Harold, another of Booth's

Booth spent almost two weeks on the run. Union troops finally tracked him to a barn in Virginia. The soldiers set the barn on fire, hoping the flames would force out Booth. Then one soldier fired and hit Booth in the neck. The soldiers pulled him from the building. Booth died a few hours later.

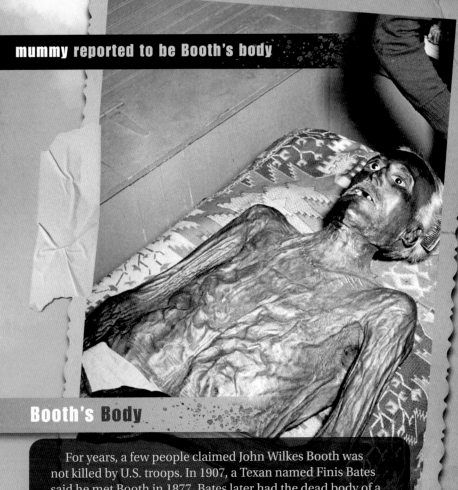

mummy reported to be Booth's body

Booth's Body

For years, a few people claimed John Wilkes Booth was not killed by U.S. troops. In 1907, a Texan named Finis Bates said he met Booth in 1877. Bates later had the dead body of a person turned into a mummy. He said the mummy was Booth. He took the mummy all over the country. In 1993, a writer said Bates' story was true. He wanted to see who was really buried in Booth's grave. The writer asked a court for permission to dig up Booth's grave. The court refused. Although rumors still exist, today most people believe Booth is buried in the grave.

ALGER HISS

1904 – 1996

During World War II (1939–1945), the Soviet Union, Great Britain, and the United States were **allies**. But the Americans and British didn't trust the Soviets' **communist** government. The Soviets didn't trust the Americans or the British either. Some Americans feared the Soviets were spying on the U.S. government. The traitor Alger Hiss fueled those fears.

Hiss was a communist, but few people knew it. Hiss worked for the U.S. State Department, which handles relations with foreign countries. In 1933, he secretly began spying for the Soviet Union. Hiss gave the Soviets details about U.S. efforts to stop Soviet spies. He also gave them information about private talks held between the United States and its allies.

ally

a person or country that gives support to another

communist

relating to communism; communism is a way of organizing a country so the land, houses, and businesses belong to the government and the profits are shared by all.

In 1948, Whittaker Chambers accused Hiss of spying. Chambers had helped Hiss spy for the Soviets. Hiss denied Chambers' claim, even though Chambers had notes that Hiss had written for the Soviets. In 1950, Hiss was found guilty of lying in court. Until his death, he continued to say he had never spied.

Whittaker Chambers

The Hiss case made some Americans distrust anyone who was not strongly against communism. The case also led to a new law making it easier to charge people with spying years after they actually spied.

THE CAMBRIDGE FIVE

- **Anthony Blunt**   1907 – 1983
- **Guy Burgess**   1911 – 1963
- **John Cairncross** 1913 – 1995
- **Donald Maclean** 1913 – 1983
- **Kim Philby**   1912 – 1988

In the 1930s, some people in Great Britain supported the Soviet Union's communist goals. Five men who went to England's Cambridge University became spies for the Soviets. They are sometimes called the Cambridge Five.

Anthony Blunt

Donald Maclean

decode

to turn something that is written in code into ordinary language

During World War II, John Cairncross **decoded** secret German messages for the British. Cairncross secretly passed them on to the Soviets.

Starting in 1944, Donald Maclean worked for the British in Washington, D.C. He knew about British and American efforts to develop **atomic bombs**. He gave this information to the Soviets.

Anthony Blunt, Guy Burgess, and Kim Philby were British intelligence officers. They gave the Soviets details about British efforts to spy on the Soviet Union.

atomic bomb blast

Together, these five men helped the Soviet Union develop its own atomic weapons program. They also told the Soviets when the British and Americans knew they were being spied upon.

atomic bomb

a powerful bomb that explodes with great force; atomic bombs destroy large areas and leave behind dangerous radiation.

23

Philby was the most damaging of the five. In 1945, Elizabeth Bentley told U.S. officials she was a Soviet spy. Philby learned this news and told the Soviets. The Soviets warned other spies who worked with Bentley. The warning prevented these other Soviet spies from being caught. Philby also told the Soviets that one of their spies was a **double agent**. The Soviets killed the man, as well as British spies working in the Soviet Union.

Guy Burgess

Kim Philby

FACT:

During World War II, the Soviets offered the Cambridge Five money for spying. The men refused it. They wanted to help spread communism, not make money.

double agent

a spy who works for one country's spy agency but is really loyal to another

By 1951, the Americans knew several British officials were Soviet spies. Maclean was the top suspect. But Philby knew what the Americans knew and he told the Soviets. The Soviets helped Maclean and Burgess escape to the Soviet Union. Philby followed in 1963. The Soviets told Blunt to go too, but he refused. He had little contact with the Soviets after 1951.

Cambridge campus

Cairncross was almost caught by the British government. He admitted to giving the Soviets some information, but he denied being a spy. The British didn't arrest him, but they told him to leave the country. The Cambridge Five spy ring was broken.

KLAUS FUCHS

1911 – 1988

During World War II, Klaus Fuchs was a talented scientist helping the United States build an atomic bomb. He was also a communist spying for the Soviet Union.

Fuchs thought the Soviet Union needed atomic weapons to defend itself. He passed secrets to the Soviets while working on atomic weapons in England. He continued to spy after he began research in the United States. In 1945, he gave the Soviets detailed plans for making an atomic bomb. Later, he sent secrets about the even deadlier hydrogen bomb.

Meanwhile, Fuchs didn't know that Americans had broken a secret Soviet code. By 1948, the Americans knew Fuchs was a spy. He was back in England when British officials questioned him. He confessed to spying.

Fuchs spent nine years in prison for his crime. His spying helped the Soviets build new weapons faster than they could have on their own.

atomic bomb being tested

FACT:

Fuchs passed secrets to a man he only knew as Raymond. Before they first met, Raymond told Fuchs to carry a tennis ball. Raymond said he would carry a pair of gloves. These items would help them identify each other.

THE ROSENBERGS

- **Julius Rosenberg** 1918 – 1953
- **Ethel Rosenberg** 1915 – 1953

In the early 1950s, Julius and Ethel Rosenberg filled the news. The married couple was found guilty of spying. Although they always denied their guilt, they were **executed** for their crime.

During World War II, the Rosenbergs were communists. Julius wanted to help the Soviet Union. He asked other American communists to help him contact Soviet spies. The Soviets then began using him as a spy. Ethel was not actively involved in this espionage, but she knew what her husband was doing.

execute

to kill someone as punishment for a crime

Julius knew scientists were creating an atomic bomb in New Mexico. Ethel's brother, David Greenglass, got a job at the Los Alamos National Laboratory where the bomb was being built. He agreed to become a spy too. He gave Julius information about the bomb. Julius passed the information to the Soviets.

In 1950, U.S. officials caught Greenglass. But by this time, the Soviets had built their own atomic weapons. They had been helped by the secrets they received from U.S. spies.

Los Alamos National Laboratory

FACT:

The Rosenberg spy ring gave the Soviets information that helped them build radar equipment, jet engines, computers, and a special kind of fuse. Years later, some of this technology helped the Soviets shoot down a U.S. spy plane.

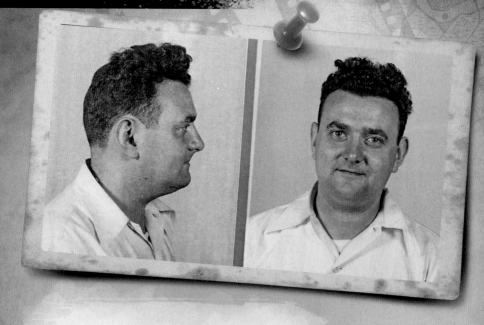

Greenglass admitted to being a spy and told authorities about Julius' role in the spy ring. Both Rosenbergs were soon arrested. At trial, they denied they were spies. But they were found guilty and sentenced to death.

The Rosenbergs fought their verdict in other courts. Some people believed they were not spies. Others said Ethel should not be killed because she had not actually spied. But Greenglass and his wife, Ruth, said Ethel had typed information to send to the Soviets. To the jury, this fact proved her guilt. The Rosenbergs were sent to the electric chair in 1953. Neither one ever admitted guilt.

Years after the trial, David Greenglass said he and his wife had lied about Ethel's typing of notes. They agreed to lie about her role so the government would not arrest Ruth.

demonstrators pleading for the Rosenbergs' release

Finding Proof

Questions about the Rosenbergs' guilt lasted for decades. Finally, in the 1990s, new evidence proved Julius was a spy. A former Soviet official admitted he had been Julius' contact. The U.S. government also released information it had collected during World War II. The information came from secret Soviet messages. The messages showed Julius' spy activities. Finally, in 2008, a spy who had worked with Julius admitted his own guilt for the first time. The spy, Morton Sobell, also said Julius was a spy.

rudolf abel

1903 – 1971

After World War II, the United States and the Soviet Union had a conflict of ideas known as the cold war. During this time, the Soviets sent agents to work with spymasters in the United States. A spymaster's job was to collect secret information from other Soviet spies.

One of the most famous spymasters was Rudolf Abel. Abel was born in England. His family moved to the Soviet Union when he was 21. In 1948, the Soviets sent him to the United States to spy. With his good English speaking skills, Abel pretended he was a U.S. citizen in New York. In addition to collecting information from other Soviet spies, he also tried to recruit new spies.

Rudolf Abel (center)

In 1957, a Soviet agent working with Abel turned himself over to U.S. officials. He offered to tell them everything he knew if they would let him live in the United States. Abel was arrested, found guilty, and ordered to serve 30 years in jail. His arrest was a major blow to Soviet spying activities in the United States.

Abel later proved useful to the United States. In 1960, the Soviet Union shot down a U.S. spy plane and captured its pilot. Two years later, the Soviets agreed to give back the pilot in exchange for Abel. The former spy returned to the Soviet Union.

Spy Gear

Abel used hollow coins and bolts, as well as other items, to send and receive secret messages. These devices looked natural for a person to carry. When he was arrested, the FBI also found special cameras and code-writing pads.

Today, spies continue to use secret devices to gather and send information. Tiny video cameras are snaked under doors or through key holes to peek into rooms. Small electronic devices called bugs are used to listen in on private conversations. Microdot cameras shrink photographs of secret codes and documents. The pictures are so small that they can be hidden in hollow rings or coins. The documents must be read with a magnifying glass.

THE WALKER SPY RING

- **John Walker Jr.**   1937 –
- **Arthur Walker**   1934 –
- **Michael Walker**   1962 –
- **Jerry Whitworth**   1939 –

As the United States fought the Vietnam War (1959–1975), its enemies received help from the Soviet Union. The Soviets received their own help from John Walker Jr., a U.S. traitor.

John Walker Jr. (left)

In 1967, Walker was in the U.S. Navy, and he wanted to make more money. He decided to sell information about Navy codes to the Soviet Union. With these codes, the Soviets learned which targets Navy planes were going to bomb in Vietnam. The Soviets told the Vietnamese so they could move soldiers and supplies before the bombs hit.

Walker soon recruited other spies. The first was his friend Jerry Whitworth. Then Walker recruited his brother Arthur and son Michael. The Walker spy ring lasted until 1985. They helped the Soviets read several million secret U.S. messages.

Over the years, the Walker spy ring received at least $1 million from the Soviets. They would have kept spying if John had not angered his ex-wife. She knew he earned a lot of money spying. Angered that Walker wouldn't give her money that he owed her, she told the government about Walker's spying. This information led to his arrest.

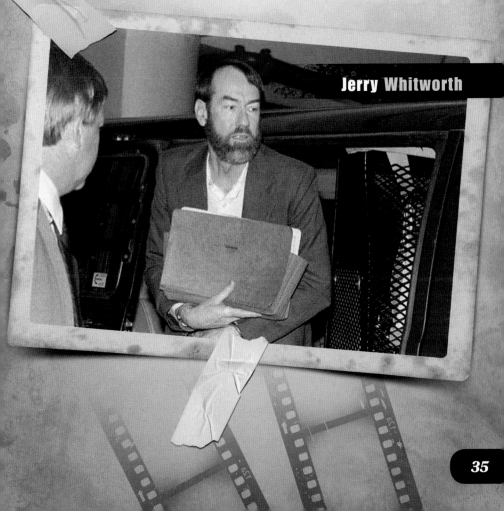

Jerry Whitworth

After they were caught, the three older spies were sentenced to life in prison. John Walker agreed to tell the government all he knew about the spy ring if Michael got a lighter sentence. The younger Walker was released from prison in 2000.

Michael Walker

FACT:

John Walker said he had thought about killing his ex-wife so she could never reveal his espionage.

ROBERT HANSSEN

1944 –

During the cold war, Robert Hanssen's job was to help catch Soviet spies. Instead, he betrayed his country. As a teen, Hanssen read about the life of British spy Kim Philby. He later decided that he wanted to be the greatest spy ever. Hanssen also knew that it could make him extra money. He didn't care that he'd be betraying his own country.

Hanssen joined the Federal Bureau of Investigation (FBI) in 1976. He spent most of his time working in **counterintelligence**. He knew how the United States tried to catch Soviet spies. Hanssen also learned about Soviet double agents who secretly helped the Americans.

counterintelligence
work done to stop other spies from stealing secrets

In 1979, Hanssen gave the Soviets the name of a double agent. Later he sent the Soviets important classified papers. He did not tell the Soviets his name. But they could tell he worked for a U.S. intelligence agency.

Hanssen loved being a double agent. He received $600,000 in cash and diamonds for giving the Soviets top secret information.

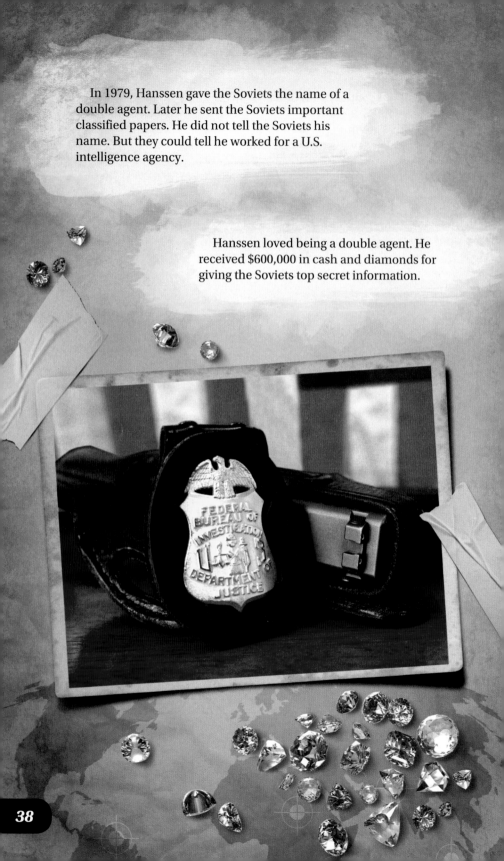

While he was with the FBI, Hanssen studied Soviet spying activities. He learned how the United States tried to prevent them. At times he saw information from every U.S. intelligence agency. Hanssen had permission to read almost all secret government papers. He learned about American military plans and the newest U.S. weapons.

With this information, the Soviets could improve their own weapons. They also knew in advance what the United States would do if the two nations went to war.

FACT:

To hide who he was, Hanssen signed his letters to the Soviets as "Ramon Garcia." He also used the name "Jim Baker." Soviet intelligence officers simply referred to him as "B."

Over the years, Hanssen gave the Soviets thousands of documents and computer files. He left some papers at a park in Virginia. The Soviets picked up the papers at this **dead drop** site and left him money.

Robert Hanssen's family

During the 1980s and 1990s, Hanssen continued spying. At the same time, he seemed like a loyal American. Meanwhile, the FBI knew there was a **mole** in U.S. intelligence. Yet no one knew that Hanssen was the double agent.

dead drop

a secret location where spies can leave messages and gear for another spy

mole

a spy who works within the government of a country but who supplies secret information to another country

Finally, a Soviet spy sold information to the FBI about Hanssen. The agency watched Hanssen and saw him at dead drop sites. The FBI arrested him in February 2001.

FBI agent searching Hanssen's mail

Hanssen could have been executed for his crimes. Instead, the government sent him to prison for life. In return, Hanssen had to tell the government everything about his spying activities. Hanssen remains in a high-security prison. He was the most dangerous spy in FBI history.

Death of Double Agents

Some of the most damaging information Robert Hanssen revealed was about Soviet double agents. Based partly on what he told them, Soviet officials arrested and executed at least three of these agents. Another spent several years in prison. All together, Hanssen revealed the names of 50 people who either worked for the United States or were asked to give the country information.

ALDRICH AMES

1941 –

During the cold war, the United States used the Central Intelligence Agency (CIA) to spy on the Soviets. Aldrich Ames was a CIA agent. Instead of working against the Soviets, Ames betrayed his country to help them.

In 1985, Ames decided to become a traitor to pay off large debts. He revealed the names of 25 Soviets working for the CIA and FBI. The Soviet government arrested them and killed at least ten of them. Some of the people Ames betrayed were co-workers or friends. He also told the Soviets about secret devices the Americans used to gather information. Over the years, Ames earned more than $2 million for spying.

The CIA and FBI learned that some Soviet agents working for them were being executed. The CIA began searching for disloyal officers. Ames' new wealth made him a suspect, but he continued his spying.

I AM READY TO MEET AT B ON 1 OCT. I CANNOT READ NORTH 13-19 SEPT. IF YOU WILL MEET AT B ON 1 OCT. PLS SIGNAL NORTH OF 20 SEPT TO CONFI. NO MESSAGE AT PIPE. IF YOU CANNOT MEE 1 OCT, SIGNAL NORTH AFTER 27 SEPT WITH MESSAGE AT PIPE.

In 1993, the FBI began to investigate Ames. They found documents in his home linking him to the Soviet Union. Ames was arrested and sentenced to life in prison. He remains the worst mole ever to work for the CIA.

FACT:

Ames' wife Rosario was arrested with him. She knew about his spying and sometimes helped him. She was sentenced to five years in jail.

JOHN WALKER LINDH

1981 –

On September 11, 2001, **terrorists** used commercial airplanes to attack the World Trade Center in New York City and the Pentagon in Arlington, Virginia. They also caused an airplane to crash in Pennsylvania. These terrorists belonged to a group known as al-Qaida. Their leader was based in Afghanistan. U.S. military forces went there to find him. Once there, they found Californian John Walker Lindh fighting for al-Qaida.

As a teen, Lindh became a Muslim. He traveled overseas to study his new religion. He was devoted to his faith. He also wanted to help Muslim terrorists fighting in Pakistan. After receiving military training there, he went to Afghanistan. He ended up at an al-Qaida training camp. Members of al-Qaida worked with a group of religious students called the Taliban. Lindh knew both groups opposed the United States.

terrorist

a person who uses violence and threats to get something from a group of people or a government

After the September 11 attacks, Lindh and other al-Qaida members prepared to battle U.S. forces and their Afghan allies. The Taliban was quickly defeated. In November, Lindh was captured.

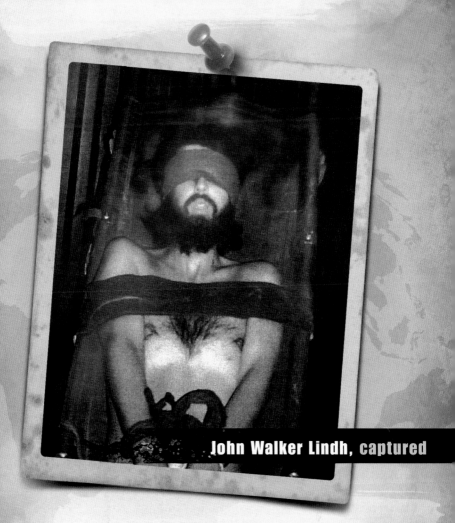

John Walker Lindh, captured

Lindh was brought to the United States and charged with conspiracy to kill U.S. citizens. He admitted to a lesser crime of helping the Taliban. Lindh was sent to prison for 20 years. His case fueled fears that Americans could never be sure who was a terrorist or a traitor.

GLOSSARY

ally (AL-eye) — a person or country that gives support to another

atomic bomb (uh-TOM-ik BOM) — a powerful bomb that explodes with great force; atomic bombs destroy large areas and leave behind dangerous radiation.

communist (KOM-yuh-nist) — relating to communism; communism is a way of organizing a country so the land, houses, and businesses belong to the government and the profits are shared by all.

conspiracy (kuhn-SPIHR-uh-see) — a secret, illegal plan that a group of people makes

counterintelligence (koun-tur-in-TEL-uh-juhnss) — work done to stop other spies from stealing secrets

court-martial (KORT-MAR-shuhl) — a military trial

dead drop (DED DROP) — a secret location where spies can leave messages and gear for another spy

decode (dee-KODE) — to turn something that is written in code into ordinary language

disciple (duh-SYE-puhl) — someone who follows the teachings of a leader

double agent (DUH-buhl AY-juhnt) — a spy who works for one country's spy agency but is really loyal to another

execute (EK-suh-kyoot) — to kill someone as punishment for a crime

loyalist (LOI-uh-list) — a colonist who was loyal to Great Britain during the Revolutionary War

mole (MOHL) — a spy who works within the government of a country but who supplies secret information to another country

patriot (PAY-tree-uht) — a person who sided with the colonists during the Revolutionary War

terrorist (TER-ur-ist) — a person who uses violence and threats to get something from a group of people or a government

treason (TREE-zuhn) — the crime of betraying your country by spying for another country or by helping an enemy during a war

read more

Blake, Spencer. *Spyology: The Complete Book of Spycraft.* Cambridge, Mass.: Candlewick Press, 2008.

Burgan, Michael. *Spying and the Cold War.* On the Front Line. Chicago: Raintree, 2006.

Martin, Michael. *Spy Gear.* Spies. Mankato, Minn.: Capstone Press, 2008.

Stewart, James. *Spies and Traitors.* North Mankato, Minn.: Smart Apple Media, 2008.

Internet Sites

FactHound offers a safe, fun way to find Internet sites related to this book. All of the sites on FactHound have been researched by our staff.

Here's all you do:

Visit *www.facthound.com*

FactHound will fetch the best sites for you!

INDEX